Some

Prairie Schooner Book Prize in Poetry | EDITOR: *Kwame Dawes*

Always

Are

JIHYUN YUN

Hungry

UNIVERSITY OF NEBRASKA PRESS   LINCOLN

Acknowledgments for the use of copyrighted
material appear on pages 67–70, which
constitute an extension of the copyright page.

Library of Congress
Cataloging-in-Publication Data
Names: Yun, Jihyun, author.
Title: Some are always hungry / Jihyun Yun.
Description: University of Nebraska Press, 2020.
Series: Prairie Schooner Book Prize in Poetry
Identifiers: LCCN 2020004233
ISBN 9781496222183 (paperback)
ISBN 9781496223623 (epub)
ISBN 9781496223630 (mobi)
ISBN 9781496223647 (pdf)
Subjects: LCGFT: Poetry.
Classification: LCC PS3625.U526 S66 2020
DDC 811/.6—dc23
LC record available at
https://lccn.loc.gov/2020004233

Set in Adobe Garamond by Laura Buis.
Designed by N. Putens.

For my mother & her mother & hers

Of wisdom, splendid columns of light
waking sweet foreheads,
I know nothing

but what I've glimpsed in my most hopeful of daydreams
of a world without end,
amen

       —Li-Young Lee

CONTENTS

SOME ARE ALWAYS HUNGRY

All Female

At the night markets, women
peddle their prices, shout in swift
Cantonese over gurgling tanks
of sea spawn: snails, young eels born
for smoke, coal, skewers. The blood
clams loll, tongues over shell lips
as we buy a bag of cockles
and three crabs, sweet with egg.
Their claws beg, puncture holes
in the cherry red, *Please come again.*
At home, my women crack them open,
cleave the lip's hem, plunge
and snap. The men watch game shows
as we wreck the girl bodies
for roe, and I don't know why.

They are always sweeter, more pricey,
Halmeoni says, pulling the last
claw from the last crab, stumps
still writhing in the sink. She dismantles
the breast next and what pulsates
inside is all gully and wet.

It's always the girls. For everything.
When was the last time you've heard
of rooster soup? We put the bodies
to boil in salt and broth.

Outside, the winter
interrogates, our windows
fogged. If our feast ever happens,
if time has not misplaced us,
may these girls rise violet
from the pot, untangle their legs
from perilla and leek
and make for the sea
with their limbs in their teeth.

My Grandmother Thinks of Love while Steeping Tea

Though you won't be sated
let me adore you in my way:

dried persimmons to tear into,
the flesh yields: a sparrow's wing.

Coat your lip with pulp and sugar
from tea boiled in the copper pot I loved

to bruise over patient flames. The ginger
sharp and sweet, will permeate our palm's

ravines. I'll wait until the water golds, then yuja rind,
coiled cinnamon, clove, dates like sun

worn faces. Drink it all,
dredge the bottom for sunk honey

pull the thumb of ginger into your mouth
and suck. I mean for you to taste

your inheritance. The gunpowder,
our soil.

Passage, 1951

Once, I saw shrapnel cut
a woman's head clean
off like a halved pill bug.
Her legs kept carrying her
a while, from this world
into the next,
and when she finally
succumbed, the baby
strapped to her back
tumbled out like a squash
during good harvest.
The baby still lived,
but no one stopped
but to undress the mother,
press her bared body into earth,
take what they could for themselves.
I did too. My siblings and I, a plague
of locust on each new body
that folded. We fought others off
with disrobed hunger,
all teeth and tremor.
I feared we would never
un-wild ourselves.

But this way, at least,
we were fed.
A few pouches
of stolen grains or a strip of jerky
still damp with sweat.
We grew to love the iron
in death. My sister began to smile
while looting bodies,
and the sight of her
put freeze in me.
It was only after seeing her
I knew what my own
mouth was doing.

Bone Soup, 1951

Into the red hot roil we spill,
backs flecked with the wrecking
heat. By fucking the farmer
we received two chunks of calf leg
bones to put to boil. Starved for days,
we siphon off the fat froth,
coat our split lips with it. The broth
is hot, white, and saltless, sucked
as if from a breast. The farmer's barn
is gutted now, we've heard his last chickens
were slain—entrails snapped up
to stay the fat hunger.

For Now, Nothing Burns

Stir the root life of a withered people. Call them from their houses, and teach them to dream.

  —Jean Toomer, *Cane*

Say our bodies can forget
       the ash
Say jet plane thunder is merely a reminder
    to wake.
The people strewn around us are not
people   only reservoirs
        pumping into one great vein.
What's spilled is a river
      we must follow.
Safety is not far,

            stand up.
  The dust plumes block light
        but not the morning's arrival.
Sister   I believe we will never die.
   See

      the bright lamps of our whole bodies

      Call it sanctuary,
call us lotus
  we bloom   in rot
    rise bog-bodied

        into tomorrow.

When we get there
                    I will beg for rations
feed you corn syrup
                              spoonful after sweet
        mournful spoonful.

Diptych of Girl in 1953

Baby brother, I've counted coins
under a fat apple moon as soldiers
scraped skin off the rocks outside.
Your tuition in hand, I am naked
as dusk. The husk of my hanbok
unfurled before a flag whose stars
I've laid under—stunned
      night after night.

Somehow I was a virgin before this.

They call me "western wife"
or rag. Is the moniker still wretched
if it becomes literally true? Soon
I will follow a white man to America,
his war-relic bride. How to tell you
without vacating all trust?

Tell me again of love
and its dark mirrors:
well-skinned pear, our cheeks
in the dust. The wet shred
of a body,

Your voice carrying
clear over the threshold,
Sister, welcome home
before you turned
to embrace me.

" "

My dear,
the war
is over.
A distant
country
tells me
we are
split.

Field Notes from My Grandparents

This ghost, I know by name.
Father, I washed your feet in a basin
of silted river before I fled
across the border.
You sat on your vast throne
of nothing, thumbed
the black snarl of my hair
you said, *Dear Jung-Hi,*
fate is a lazy man's
fever dream. Outside, fire rained.
In our village, the clot of hunger
never loosened. When I fled
without returning you
to earth, you did not resent me.
Please say it,
you did not resent me.

For a while, we were lucky.
My family was textile
and white rice rich.
The war began without me
knowing. Then jet planes
maddened the skies overhead,

prelude to blood.
prelude to human bodies,
the floods they bring. I was young,
then not. I thought to myself
O God, O God, and received only smoke.
The planes dropped their eggs,
hatched a red so loud
the landscape was struck
briefly mute.

My leg darkened with rot.
To live, I've run across the parallel
and yet—

Over the eaves, the sun is rising;
a fevered petal hung on the hurt
of daybreak, a stunned promise
you emerge from, thing
of morning.

My softened limb does not
disgust. You promise me a new day
and like an animal on your back,
    you carry me.

Blossom of the sand pear,
this woman cleaving
day open. Woman
and her weathered book bag,
her work clothes, her face,
a water-worn stone. Woman

and her hard hands. Woman
and her wounds, her eyes
that fill my throat
with loam, rich and possible.
May every flower grow
from this torn orifice. Woman
and her mouth of blades.
Her *dal-go-na* after work:
baking soda and sugar
melted into browned shapes
by street-side vendors,
woman I'll strive to love,
these *they-are-sweets*.

Despite the endless shells
that snowed the horizon,
camellias burst their laurels
the hue of a lover's cheek.
It's the blood, you say,
It hydrates. Even newly
out of war, we are afflicted
with spring. A flower grows
through the hinge of a bone,
all stem and snapdragon.

O husband, I too
am desperate.
Tell me who I am
and I will be.

Immigration

For S.J.L.

But Sun,
the salt tucked under your tongue
gains nothing in the way of mourning.
Black rock and root, you mouth
to keep your mind off it.
Morning eddies, clamped tooth
of red blown wet and tidal.
They look and see
hardly human. Hinge jaw and body,
socket and eye. I am not yet conceived,
      but inevitably—

Tell me it was worth it,
and I'll believe you.
Jaw shred raw from concrete,
occasional barbed eye
of the unforgiving hue.
When they reached,
did you think of loaches
dying between your thighs?

How they gorged and writhed
as you boiled them along the river rock
of your childhood stream, the burnished pot
frothing its reddened copper. The men will live
to callous their hands further.
Sun, in this life, I will be your daughter
        and you will teach me how to run.

Homonyms

1. 태우다 · *(T'aeuda)*
a. *To burn or singe by fire*
b. *To carry, give a ride, pick up*

I burned you. You grew up
burning, bundled on my back.
Petulant petal, jaundiced thing,
plucked from my amniotic rib.
I had you suck the milk
of dandelions to take the yellow
from your skin, sliced antlers
rendered to wretched tea
to temper your bloodied
coughing. I dislodged
your limbs in hopes
you'd grow to something
lithe and desired, the suggestion
of a girl. And you did
until your girlhood grew
dangerous as it does
for all girls. I've been sorry
ever since. You burned
on the coattails of our
immigration. Singed
your tongue on America
until no tongue was rightfully
yours, until you came home

disgraced having pissed yourself
instead of asking to go
to the restroom in English.
But I wasn't ashamed. I burned
you gently in my arms, burned
you all the way home, away
from the laughter, burned you
against my breast to safety.
And daughter, you will not
forget these aches you learned.
If you have a daughter,
you will burn her too.

I Revisit Myself in 1996

English has just begun
to bruise my tongue
but I am all Korean.
I am five.
I live in California
on Washington Street,
so I think I live
in Washington State
and dream of California
weather all sun all the time,
except at night when God
throws stars like darts and punctures
the ground sometimes.
Despite funerals,
I don't know what it is
to die so I hope ghosts
are real. Who would rather be gone
than ghost? Whoever says so
are liars. They are liars.
But enough. I am a child. I live
closer to birth than death.
Sometimes I'm a mother,
I pluck spent ham hocks

from trash cans and go outside.
I part the soil like a small Red Sea.
I've seen Halmeoni erect enough garlic
stems and carrot roots to know
how this works. I cover the bones in soil
and wait for pigs to grow.

War Soup

Ingredients

- Pork belly
- Anchovy broth
- Instant noodles
- Onion
- Garlic
- Spam
- Hot pepper paste
- American cheese
- Kimchi

1. In eight cups of boiling water, add dried kelp and anchovy, soaked shitake mushrooms and onion tops to make a broth. Grind four cloves of garlic together with hot pepper paste, soy, and sugar for seasoning. Set the mixture aside for later.

2. Onion carpeted in pork fat and rice wine flared, very briefly, an ignited landscape. Then sun-dried pepper flakes staining the oil, a sundry of roots tossed in at rough dice, zucchini cut to half-moons, halved and quartered heads of kimchi. The stock should not disappoint, heavy with anchovy and odd bits. Set it all to boil, no witness, low heat.

3. We've not long been able to afford this: life-giving flesh, singed wire hair that remembers outhouse and apple core. The fat ripples its own horizon, studded white over pink meat, cartilage wedged there where

the muscle gathers. Cut the slabs into mince, light those dented pots.

4. *Dear family I left behind*
   in the northern province of my birth,
   do you live as I feed and am fed
         have they given you to sea?

5. Then Spam, more tofu than animal, cut to cubes. Say, *we made do with what we did. At the bases, the Americans gave cans of beans or meat. We weren't picky, boiled it all with weeds and scraped carcass. We called it Johnson-tang, rejoiced like we'd never again need to eat, as if the miles were no real thing.* Now chili, now green onion sprigs.

6. The northern village of my birth, a storm-crushed window. The gaunt faces of my people parade the TV screen; dear lord, dear leader.

7. *Let the noodles wilt*
   over broth just before serving.
   At the table, over kerosene flame,
   three generations tend to the pyre
   that feeds and feeds.

   What a blessing,
   to have passed through hunger.
   I will teach my daughters
   to bare their palms.
   I will teach them how to beg.

The Daughter Transmorphic

Somewhere, the idea
of me pricks her finger
on the thorn of strange
flowers clipped from
her girlhood.
What the sap waters,
grows to a city.
I've always wanted
to populate myself.
Mama, if lore has taught
me anything, I know queendoms,
like language, can't last long
childless. Why must all
tired stories start
with an exit of the mother?
A matrilineage expunged
and covered in moths
mouthing what's left.
Flip the page. Gone
is the matriarch.

Close the book
and blood seeps
between chapters.
Now, men with bayonets.
Tomorrow, dogs. In no version
are they not hunting us.

Yellow Fever

Call down the girl from the mud-slicked mountains, pluck the evidence of August from her head of shorn kelp. This caterwauling girl, less man than animal. Cheeks smeared wild from the chokeberries she picked, brambles at the river's lip too giving. Doesn't she know the stained hand of generosity, never to trust it? Nothing is free. China doll. Baby. Some men want you prim on their knee: lips bite red. The coal hue of your eyes irrefutable. You were never meant to be American. Your root, they believe they can taste: carnal amen, rice milk and spice. A winter sunrise fogged in the land of morning calm. All imagined, but no matter. You are still a girl. With luck, the guilty ones will wait awhile. When the first blood releases between your thighs, they'll come. You were born knowing to mourn this.

Saga of the Nymph and the Woodcutter

Douse the black lacquered belly of the earthenware pot with rice vinegar antiseptic and scrub. Tonight, the girls squat taut on their haunches, peel open prone heads of cabbage, salting between each leaf and on it. As they stack the heads ten high so they can release their waters—un-tender and un-mild themselves—they recall their bodies as they were at the first descent: lips serrated, cutting grooves on their gums, brilliant and capable before the men came to claim them, stole their celestial robes so they couldn't fly home. Clipped wing of the seraphim, they say, *Baby, you can't be mad forever.*

Say, *Stay.*
Say, *Stay.*

On its blue shelf of night, the moon is a dunce. It doesn't wonder why its daughters don't return. It kills every animal that gazes too long on its light, but not the men. The girls were made wives, then mothers, bellies swelled like winter melons split too soon from a vine. They didn't want this life, they wanted—

And back again to the task at hand, the gimjang that must be finished before the day's end. Now bid the oysters yawn around the shucking blade. Now pack the brined heads with chili and jeot, the hangari is hungry. Now set the boiled pork on gilded plates before the men who laugh at the TV, frozen and golden, absorbing light like fat gods on an altar.

Fish Head Soup

Remember this: fish head soup
should be eaten on the hottest summer day.
Pungent and spicy, it will make you sweat
       keep you cool.

Boil it in a big pot with peppers and leeks
and minari leaves. Eat it cross-legged
out on the weathered wooden porch like we did.

There is little of the head that cannot
be eaten. Pull away the cheeks,
the meat there is tender and sweet.
The eyes should be shared.
Suck the skin off sheets of cartilage
and when picking flesh off the jaw,
don't snag your thumb on their teeth.

Halmeoni sorts bones on the splayed newspapers.
There's been another shooting in Oakland
and she lays the prickly spines across obituaries.
This is how we go, she says as she points
at the picked clean faces,
the shucked-out sockets.

Recipe

닭도리탕

Ingredients
- Whole chicken
- Soy sauce
- Onion
- Carrots
- Potatoes
- Red pepper flakes
- Red pepper paste
- Sugar

1. Splay the hen on the cutting board's yellowed face. With a well-loved blade, caress the goosed skin off and most of the fat. Leave just enough to render and coat the bottom of the pot.

2. For sauce: garlic crushed by the flat end of a knife, soy, ground pepper flakes, and paste. Measurements: pinches between fingertips, vague spoonfuls, whatever muscle memory dictates or does not. Any sort of sweetness: sugar/corn syrup/honey. Set aside the mixture or later.

3. *Peel the ninjin*, Grandma says in Japanese, though she means danggeun, or "carrot" in Korean. She mistakes the two often, so I know what she means. The skin curls beneath the paring knife's persuasion, as I think of colonization via inheritance, via memory. These words I've no reason to know but do.

4. (A tongue, cleaved with trying.)

5. Add rough cuts of carrot, onion, potatoes. Now ginger and garlic ground to pungent pith. Cover it all with water and seasoning sauce, wait for it to thicken, inelegant as most good food is.

6. She calls the stew dakdoritang, despite controversy. Some believe it translates roughly into "chicken-chicken stew," dak meaning "chicken" in Korean, dori derived from the Japanese: *tori* (bird). A slim silhouette of occupation tethered to our language like a haunting. Others say this is not true. Rather they posit the etymological root of dori lies in 도려 내다, "to cut out or discard." These arguments feel so far from me, yet after decades come and gone, Grandma cannot discard Japanese. She says *tamanegi* for yangpa, *shio* for sogeum, as if to remind how close we came to erasure. Our tongues boiled down to language, broth skimmed of birth fat.

7. *During occupation, this tongue was dangerous, but still we wanted to keep it. We met under bridges to flex our Korean. In the quiet and moonlight. Under cicadas and sound-swell. With hands clasped. Once, I watched an imperial soldier cave a man's face in for refusing to give up our mother tongue. The soldier's own face gave away nothing. When I was bad, mother said the Japanese would come and get me. I didn't fear demons lurking in dark corners of our room, only other Asian faces.*

8. She reaches into the bowl to claim the throat. The spine curved down as if caught in a moment of prayer. Soon it's laid bare, just sinew and ridged bone. Chili studded, stained red, she licks her fingers clean.

Diptych of Animal and Womb

These wombs belong to us, not the idiot creatures they are attached to. They were given to us by God to reproduce ourselves with. We need to look for ways to get these stupid animals to give us back the wombs they have stolen from us.
    —Posted to r/braincels, Reddit

I.

what flurry of knives / what small gods beasting through the needlegrass and thorn-thistle / whipping the deerflies into such fury / what rare stones inside me / what tessellating skin / animal and performance / what nephrite and bug glint / blood mad and hunger / whose womb wounds who / not you / not you / what clot of hair and meat unzipped to sunset / Poacher, what joy tears your face into a h(a)unting / To you, the body: abstraction / cruelty: abstraction / the knife slips past the pelt / a pulsing city lifted from my belly / What beast would gift me this body and name itself God / what borrowed rib and rain / what stories / what claim over that which grows / in another /

II.

You, grinning as you squalor
your hands on my meat.
Nothing has been won.
This city, I will evacuate
until my ruler wakes.

Aubade

So warm the nights
of plum wine and fruit
on your disrobed bed,
mattress shucked bare
but for our bodies
and the wool-whiskered
blanket you cherished because
I'd bled on it once.

I said I'll never understand,
which remains true
but I still miss the moment
arrested. Your walls awash with blues
your wide windows opened to crushes
of milkweed, sage, morning glories
bittersweet as your tongue

unhusked. I couldn't bear
to look at you. Your mouth
enveloping the bottle's lip
entire, your jaw when you chewed,
the muscle there. The way you tore
into clementines with your thumbs

pushing pungent pith
in and apart.

I covered my breasts with a sheet,
but you pulled it away, bared
everything. Outside, the night
swelled and lulled, livid
with cicadas. Back then,
we weren't made for tenderness,
though swathed in summer
we fooled ourselves.

Mother Undresses

Look, she says and lifts her shirt
her bare back bent like a fishhook
riddled with scars, mostly burns
or bug bites, but of what origin are these?
The long stretches of gnarled skin
catching lamplight like the inside
of an abalone shell, running up
and down her thighs. I'm surprised
I've never known them but she
withholds so many things. She's a little
beside herself, pulling her breasts aside
observing her belly and legs. *Look
what the fever did*, so I look
and see her, mottled gosling
thing, covered with blood-red
bloomings she calls yeol-kott, "flowers
of fever." Flowers of contagion
that have rendered her
grotesque. *That bastard, that bastard*
she says as I draw her oatmeal bath
and remember she means the fever.

Blood Type

A

While spinning the skin
off an apple I nick my thumb, taste
my tannins: sweet and undeniable.

So much like my mother,
No wonder mosquitos can't
keep away.

We slick our legs with cinnamon oil,
eucalyptus, citrus rinds to alleviate
the bites raising landscapes on our thighs

But still, such embarrassing joy, these nights
of fed resignation, sikkhae we drink too quick
sugaring our tongues with rice and nectar.

The spiral wick burns down to an eye
as we scratch, red globes blooming
through our cotton pants.

AB

Tired of releasing them, my friend begins seizing
the mice, the trap's spring too cheap to kill,

and strikes them against the wall. It's awful, their eyes
bulging red, cherries between teeth.

Once, I find him drowning one in the sink,
its claws scrabble across porcelain.
Not wanting to watch it go limp, I turn away
and he says he was curious how long it would take.

B

Sometimes without warning, I'm there.
In his blue room, in the blue dusk where he wakes me
again. I feign sleep when I feel his reaching.
Acknowledge when he pants, my throat hurts.
Outside his window, the moon looks too whole. I want
to pull it through a sieve. The fractured light, something wounded
to own. Hadn't mother warned me of men
of his type, B the mercurial, B the bad boy.
When I feel him rising against my thigh, I know he is a man
of God. He only comes to claim the rib I've borrowed.

O,

the ways we treat the body.

Lilith

Nights of amniotic dark so thick I can barely see through. On our bed of loam and animal bone, you purple your mouth on mine. All I taste is bellflower, though the eyes confess it is blood. *How does it feel to be the reason I fall?* You spit at where I open, your Revelations dog tag, a carved silver sun hung around an apple-seed throttle. Its words cast shadows on my breast: "These are the ones who have not been defiled with women . . . who follow the lamb wherever he goes." But lord, our waters and flesh, the body's benediction that swells and thrashes. // A blue wind whips the aspen beyond the window. Command it to be silent // Your hands, an ember on my throat, you say, *You're mine, you're mine*, litany desperate as the labor of your hips. Dear God of man's waste, I know I'll leave this place hungry.

Husband Stitch

> Dr.—.——— was called upon to explain the "Husband Stitch," which he did
> as follows: He said that when he was stitching up a ruptured perineum, of a
> married lady, the husband . . . peeped over his shoulders and said, "Dr., can't
> you take another stitch?" and he did, and called it the "Husband Stitch."
>
> —From "Transactions of the Texas State Medical Association, Volume 17"

so my lord laid me down on her meat—
and named me her husband's—
said   *you will improve the woman's*—
well-being   I willed it so—
pearled thread through her perineum   tenderly I—
tucked into that rain—
ravaged terrain pulled taut these walls—
for her own sake   which is synonymous—
with her husband's   girlish aperture I loved—
to breathless   *you will improve*—
will increase   vulvular and sweet—
I was the opposite—
                    of violence—
            for weeks, we lived in love—
        no blood leaving unbidden   I grew—
human(e)ly fond of her body, which I wore as my own—
then her husband entered the sutured gate—
            aurora borealis broken   leaking light—
                    her rupture—
        is not my fault—
                        O tell me   oh—
tell me how to keep   sun from spilling—
        from all my man-made seams—

The woman's well-being—
born to be split   plum skinned—
        useless—

              maker   let me retell the story—
     as it should have been   a girl comes to your office—
and leaves as split as she's come   she isn't—
         punished for the gasping birth in her arms—
             seeks permission from no one for her mother wound—
        what her womb dares to do—
O unwed me from this   stitch and tremor—

                       O tight O tight O terror—
    torn there where my thread unthatched—
will improve the woman's well-being—
            will improve the woman's—
well-being—   *will improve the woman—*
      say honor, say horror—

                  I do I do I do I do—

The Tale of Janghwa and Hongryeon

Mother dreamt of roses growing between her thighs. She pulled one out and named it me. Mother dreamt of a red lotus wet with breast milk. She clipped its stem and named it my sister. For years, we grew in love. Father brought lacquered jars of honey, swiped our lips with the golden sap. Seeing the first of our breasts emerge, he said, *Sweet daughters, stay young awhile*. In response, mother dreamt of lilies breaking open, their creases curling toward sky. She dreamt this and died without witness in the night.

*

And we stepped into woman skins, though father hoped we never would. Our bodies called too many men down to our village, beckoned too much rain. *We'll be paupers after their dowries are paid*. Eyes full of thorn, Stepmother ordered her eldest son to bring her a rat. With a needle, she stabbed through its heart, cut it from its mange-melted pelt. Meat of the shucked blood clam, it glistened in her hand, under candle flame quiver, between my legs, where Stepmother placed it. Outside, the cicadas watched the blood soak a wet sun through the sheets. Hands clasped, Lotus and I slept and dreamt of nothing.

*

Dawn breaking open, a starved mouth I fall into. It is not the sun that wakes me, but Father pulling the blankets back. *Oh*, he says as if around a mouthful of salt, *Oh*. The skinned rat curled like a human in the sheets, the white-hook of Stepmother's barely withheld smile. *The whore is not yet wed and has already miscarried.* Too many eyes raking my skin, I run. The lake opens and receives.

*

        My body   *glutted blue*

the black stone of   *my uneaten eye*

                 Lotus   *I didn't mean to die*

       I merely saw   *our mother reflected*

in the water   *and bent to embrace her*

           In this lake   *I dream of water lilies*

      I cut one from its stalk   *and place it inside*

             Dear sister

      I am ready

                to bloom as I am

Caught

a girl mired in a net

between her legs   a quiver

of taking   she wants to untangle

her limbs   split the fishhook

from the soft meat of her mouth

skeleton flower

pale vein

when wet   she is briefly vanished

but that girl was me

nineteen   your red sheets redder

where whetted

with whiskey

what to do with this memory?

worked open

silt in my gills   trout mouth puckered and shut

the lazy turns of the ceiling fan

a thread of moonlight   sang opal

in your one white hair   I was frenzied by the moon

what a good girl

he must have loved having you

just like this

outside the olive trees quivered   overtaken by fruit

my girl is frigid   but you—

if wet, was I

complicit?

dear poison

dear quiver of unmaking

if I drank what you offered

if I let you hook your thumb against my lip

if my memory of that night flexes image like a convex mirror

then is memory wrong when it says I said no

only once?

some hours   you were slow hands

other times animal and ravenous

my legs caught in your sheets

like refusal

rain-wet pavement   walking home

some nights I dream of only water

Menstruation Triptych

I.

Happy to be bleeding,
I fold the unused
test into the black hem
of my pocket just to carry
this solitude with me.
Seedless belly, beloved
fallow, I.

Happy to be bleeding,
I treat myself to sangria
and ice cream, weave
flowers of invasive
species in my hair,
sing praises to Korean
over-the-counter BC.

At home, I'm so happy
to be bleeding, I pummel
my stomach against
the kitchen counter,
just in case. I know
it doesn't work
that way, but he came without

permission and inside.
I'm irrational is what I mean.

Bloodless, others fly
to nearby countries to terminate
but I'm too woman, too poor.

Lord, in this life I'll happily
bleed and bleed. Let the
animals gnaw through every
door. Let the tides overpower.

II.

She's never wanted to mother though the world demands from her nothing else. She holds the napkin to her girlhood, watches the cerise leech into the quilted fabric. Thank heavens for periods, the rivers they carve into their beds of mortal meat. Tissue blossoms. Blood tea. Thirteen, she is my mother, thinking of the fabled student, years ago, who was never taught menstruation. Who thought the red escaping her human aperture was a sign of fatal illness, wrote a letter to her mother, and took her own life. *Forgive me Mom, I don't want to die slow. I'm sorry. I'm sorry.* In a world of men, this is the cost of blood. Why let girls bleed without telling them what it means? Why bloody your hands on another's blood-body journey? She wraps the cloth close to her blood-body, draining the day closed. She thinks, *Praise this act of escaping.* Please live freely in this blood vine of your singular life. In time, I will lodge myself within you and halt the cycle, the napkin still white between your thighs. I know I will not be worth it, but somewhere, it is written. Beloved, was I selfish to come merely as I am?

III.

Here, it is not my cycle that bleeds

me, but my lover tearing through
before I am ready. It should have
mattered when he didn't care
about my pain, but in love,
I love even the wounds.
Evening primrose open
beyond the window, lifting
their stamens toward the night.

I understand.
The organic green tangle I am
also blooms best under moonlight.
Six moons from now, I won't be here
anymore. I'll be in New York scalding
my tongue on diner coffee, spitting
the grinds on my plate of eggs scraped
immaculate. I'll be drunk and happy
on 32nd Street. I'll be twenty-three,
I'll finally understand all he did to me

on that blue bed. Gondolas
rocking to driftwood in my dreams.
The hurt he said I was born to eat.
My, *Stop*. And then my, *Yes*.
I bleed like girls are taught to bleed,
pretending I am fine. *I tore you
badly*, he says with pride.
He holds his reddened fingers
to my eyes to show me
what I'm made of.

Some Are Always Hungry

We pass the last chicken thigh between us,
three generations of girls at the table
scraping around a pot that dwindles
to root and broth over blue-gas flames.
Our eyes are the same, they do not stray.
It's rude to watch the hen's last migration,
her limb passed from empty bowl
to empty bowl, body having sated
no one.

Enough, Mother says, and Grandma
finally picks up the thing. She dismantles it
like a lover. Divesting it of skin, parting
the twinned bones, the flesh in tatters.
She leaves nothing: the cartilage
that cradles, the muscle, the jut of tendon,
she takes that too.

I hate to watch her eat
the way she squalls like one
just discovering plenty
and fearing she will never trust it.

Immigration

For S.J.L.

As the chrysanthemum greens wilt under chili and oil,
my young mother slips a blade through a slab of flank,
pulls silver skin from flesh in one leaf of tissue and flex.

At sixteen, she's still new to this nation that unnames her daily.
An Oriental name will drag her, they say, so she gives up Sunju for Kathy,
though the tongue-tip press of *-th-* refuses her.

She'll say *Katt-ie* for years, and sets even her teachers snickering,
the dignity of a name only the first of things taken. It's barely dawn,
the pin-prick sun not yet heaved over the horizon,

but she prepares a week's worth of lunch boxes and dinners:
salt-beef simmered in a stock of anchovy and soy, whole kkwarigochu
sing their green roulette as they braise, some mild, some blistering.

How to love in a country that teaches surrender:
tables heavy with home. Braised hen knotted in bitter greens. Candied root
of lotus. Birth names muttered over dinner so as to not forget.

Dear 선주,
be proud of what they try
to efface.

Benediction as Disdained Cuisine

Give me now
what scalds and reeks.
Give me chilis and garlic
raw. Give me dropwort,
chrysanthemum greens.
Buckwheat and tea. The bite
of a well-ripened kimchi.
Let me wrap my meat
in what others mistake
for spoil. Let me unearth months
-old jars of ponytail radish,
turned just so, and bless
rice with its sunny juices.
Give me that funk and meju pungency.
Let the fried fish stare vacuous
as I eat the reel of its body, mouth
lolling and teethed. The egg sac
nestled inside, give me that too.
Pouch of possibility, multitude and sweet.
So crisp the oil-puffed dorsal fins,
the tail fins. How good the flesh
off the cheeks, the grease off blistered
scales. Give me now what disgusts.

Grilled tongue, entrails fatly
gleaming. Fiery chicken
feet with the nails neatly trimmed.
Minutia of bone. Spit and keep eating.
Give me stink. Give me pig
skin dipped in powdered grain.
Give me krill and pickled octopus:
suckers up and gaping.
Food that makes you honor
what was killed for your sake.
Vein of the cod roe. Blistered
hair of the intact hock. Evidence
of bodies carved from.
What makes you clasp your palms
to your nose is the bell that calls in
my hunger. I don't care anymore
what you think. Give me sesame oil
and fat. Give me bloodied and raw.
The white broth of famine food.
Food made to last. To transform
with the seasons. To survive
other nations. Give me all
I avoided so long for your sake.

Give me my heritage back.
Let me suck meat off the shell
of every animal you won't eat.
Give me refuse, and I'll make it
worthy.

Praise

On 135th and Broadway,
a thumb of light
reached for me
through Harlem's milk-froth sky.
The warmth on my cheek held me
like a body I've missed.
I heard mother's voice
in the tired rumble of trains below
as I hear her in all things

weathered. Not a clear bell,
but work-worn when she rises
in the coldest swell of night to ready
for her twelve-hour days:
hands wrapped around the hot iron
eyes closed, half dreaming
of the barley fields of her youth,
sugar buns spilling their molten cores
of walnut and spice. *Be good* she'd say
each morning, though I seldom answered.

I remember how once I found her
wringing dollars in the basement

stringing them up like egg-fattened fish
drying on a laundry line.
A patron had thrown them
in the oil-slicked sink water;
Here is a tip for the little assistant.

I don't understand what a mother is,
what toothen thing lives inside
for her to take my hand,
smile proudly, say *Daughter,*
this is the richest we have been.

Thirst

Mornings of marrow and oolong oiled
mother-of-pearl from too much milk.
      This is how we heal.

Fingers sugar-tacky, we eat the day
cloudless, watch mayflies thrust upward
      to a blue the hue of thirst.

Your lip, a crushed berry, spills
its wet cerise. You say *Even this can be*
      inherited, by which you mean

be strong. Azalea and baby's breath
drop petals on the nightstand
      like fly's eggs.

Through your bent nose, your voice
mosquitos as you sing:
      Man is ship, woman is harbor.

Day by day, I gaze toward the sea.
But we are landlocked beasts.
      Mother, I too envy any selfish thing.

Homecoming

After so long the meju blocks still welcome, hanging cracked and pungent from our awning. A year of Grandmother's care packed between the grains. The velvet whiting the surface of the bricks make promise of ambrosial spoil, brings the scent of a country never mine to me in small spoonfuls. Here, a quartered sand pear soaked in soy and yyeot. Here, charcoal and hay, a red sun slit over a violently mountainous landscape.

The kitchen window we named our garden smells heavy with peat. All the apple seed and cores we shred to feed the lucky bamboo, but she won't grow more than an inch or two. Dear weathered stalk, I am just as stubborn. Though I've come and gone from this place as often as seasons, I rarely return new. The old aches are just the same.

Some things, however, I do not recognize. A knot of chives and their purple blossoms bundling over the unburnished pot. My Grandfather's hard hands attend, pleased any living thing can pass through his touch uncut. A new shadow carves Grandmother's cheek as she calls me over, her lips a down-turned trip wire, and closes my fist around a handful of toasted sesame seeds.

I thought I'd forgotten this place, how it warms without warning.

Savaging

(verb)

The ethnological term for an animal maiming or killing her own offspring. Though observed in the wild and across various species, it most severely impacts pigs bred in captivity and subjected to severe environmental stressors.

Dear daughters, when the mind leaves
it leaves swiftly. Today I woke not knowing
which country holds me or if those love
motels stringing neon cords outside my window
were those of Oakland or Seoul. I woke having
forgotten even your faces, but remembered
my hunger. What if this is all I am left with:
memories of my young body rifling through refuse
at the U.S. bases, the slow arc of a dust-bloodied moon
illuminating garbage: animal bones I picked through
for their tears of toothed sinew, wads of gum
studded with gristle and American spit. We did our best
to rinse off the dirt, but that too is sustenance.
After all, I've seen the hungry drink soups of mud
or their own vomit, and if pride serves no man,
then let us be animal, full and unmoored
from whatever shame names us human. We boiled
trash in a big pot, watched the chicle bloom
into nothing and broth, the bone's faint bouquet
of rot brought us kids to drooling. The stock boiled
itself white. We spiced it with crushed cigarette butts
and wild weeds, called it 꿀꿀이죽, or oink-oink gruel
after the swine we had become. To this day, nothing

has tasted as good. Home that evening, my eldest sister
seized me by the hair, throttled my face red for eating
American garbage. *You weren't raised like this,*
you weren't raised like this, but in a year, my sister
in all her beauty and pride would be dead. It was like
we already knew it back then, my girl body half-transformed
into a pig, screeching its pink forfeit. My sister
thrashing my wire-haired skin, weeping for all the lives
neither of us would live.

Revisitations

This is summer closing: sweet aloe drink and linger.
Plexiglas floors suspended over the wreckage
of some ancient neighborhood in what is now Mapo.

An archeological treasure, to be preserved despite fire.
Say one spark off a coal briquette kisses what it should not,
an arm of dried wood, or the lattice hem of a girl's dress,

and hypothetically we are all engulfed in flames.
Halmeoni kisses me temple to temple, eager to introduce me
to her country but like a woman of my blood,

she leads me back to ruin. *And here is where the fire
could not be contained. See where the frameworks still stand.
These were homes. These were not excavated until after war.*

Thirty years after her war, she left this country. Thirty years
after that, she is returned to nothing familiar but the tongue
stunned with striving. But unmaking is what she knows,

and so can best convey: *The fire*, she reads, *the fire*.
The Plexiglas beckons evening by illuminating what is left.
The landmark placards commemorate the blaze

and all it failed to spare: livelihoods, lives, and the bodies
that vesseled them, shimmering their vanish in white-light
relief. It is all very glamorous the way only memorials

for tragedy can be. Above us, locusts make themselves known,
blow open August with their stutter and trill. A student lights up a smoke,
taps ash over excavated remains of a city forever

ablaze in history, and I remember across the sea, California's
dry brush is burning. On television, we hear threats of whole countries
blazed to preconception and if the fires we tend end up taking us all

who will write our eulogy? *So much is changed I can hardly bear it,*
Halmeoni says as the day yields. Where there was nothing,
a mall. Where there were shanties, a bar. *Not far from here,*

I fell in love with a cigar factory heir. The building was
gray and huge. It covered everything in soot. Even our hair,
even the trees. We'd sit under the waxwing leaves

and listen to the cigar rolling machines—In dreams, I can see them
adoring the day closed with their hands of ceaseless light.
They could have been anyone. Dear lovers, dear moment in time,

inevitably you will burn, as all living things do.

But there are things even fire fails to eviscerate: morning's onset,
the suggestion of a woman unearthed among ash, all her lived loves
large or small, sown within the hems of a charred girl's dress.

The Leaving Season

All winter we slept with backs pressed against
one another. I let him fuck me, regret,
then let it happen again. Even to myself, I had no answer.
I hated how he smoked in bed, hated the weakness
he assumed I'd inherited for my sex.
I said nothing all season.

Once, we went to Seonnyeo Beach. He meant to impress me
with a boulder in the shape of a celestial woman
mourning. Praying to go home to her sisters, but to me,
really just looked like a rock. I was more taken by the ladies
at the base of her slate dress, scraping oysters the size
of thimbles into ziplock bags.

With the tides pulled back, the beach was pockmarked,
barnacles and shellfish like so many opened eyes
tanning themselves to death in the December sun.
Once, I was dubiously alive.

They're harvesting oysters, because they're going to eat them, he explained,
to which I thought, *no shit*, but said nothing. What keeps me
so afraid of wounding a man? Later, tangled up in seaweed,
we unearthed the jawbone of some beast picked clean of meat,

its weathered teeth muscled around nothing. A few meters inland,
we found its sea-swelled face as if water knowingly freed it
of its visage. I knew it was a boat offering, a prayer
for maritime safety. What other reason would an animal
head have to wander onto shore?

But all I could think of was a dream I once had of a woman with a pig's
head walking into the water. What sweetness, to enter the sea to bless
nothing but your own safe passage. I looked down at what washed up
from this dream, porous and meat against the green of dashed soju bottles.

Wire-hair whitening with sun and not yet taken by rot,
the skull and face smiled separately.

> *As a suckling,*
> *I was led to a prone teat,*
> *fed apple core and flesh scraped*
> *from the carcass of other animals like me.*
> *Forgive my indiscretion with feed,*
> *the wild hunger that drove me to partake of the meat*
> *I would one day become. I spent my days*
> *rubbing my snout against the cage, hating my mottled*
> *pink body for its deliciousness.*
> *to be desired is rarely a good thing.*
> *When I was old enough to breed, my failure*
> *to conceive earned me a bolt*
> *between the eyes. I died without fanfare, like so.*
> *My body, they halved and sent away*
> *to be drained, salted, and swung*
> *from hooks at the market.*
> *My hooves went elsewhere,*

were braised with spice and rice liquor
to an unctuous toffee-brown. All that sweet warm
fat glistening under heat lamps, hawked
with peppers and brine shrimp. It's strange
to know this world I loved, loves me best
dismembered. I watched them use me with great
dispassion. Why blame a human for his nature
which at its core is merely hunger?
Why miss the body for what it can endure?
At some point, I lost track of my head,
felt it hoisted aboard some gleaming new boat
that hastened it toward water,
all grease and alabaster. The sun
resting baldly across my scalp untethered
some live-wire longing in me. My head,
my harrowing, my little life ended
abruptly. I followed the last remnants of me
to the open expanse of a moon-stirred sea.
They blessed and implored my head
for safety before giving it to water.
The storm above unbraided leisurely.

I saw myself unbraided
apex and heat as witnessed
from above. Fear sweetens
the meat, and so explains
the violence before every
partaking. I was just a girl
in every sense, but pressed
no charges. On your pull-out
sofa-bed, you slept affrontingly

sound. Roses on your desk,
their wilting, beer-doused heads.
Roses pressed between chapters
of your girlfriend's Herman Hesse.
It shouldn't matter how I got there,
and yet—*Did you*
walk through the door
on your own two feet?
Did you kiss them first besides
the bonfire's unhusked heat?
Yes, yes. Still drunk,
I crawled to your palm
smeared mirror, pushed *The Sorrows*
of Young Werther from where it rests,
pulled off my animal face,
and forced myself to look.

Water fills every excavated cavity
buoyant with blubber and blood, it sinks
slow. Carp nibble gratefully at its cheek
cuttlefish streak by with their curious pale meat.
For a while, it resists rot. It was wrong to reject
the body, to think it wouldn't miss it.
The water eases between sinew and skull
lifting away until face and bone hurtle toward shore
divorced of each other for the lovers to find.
Do not be tricked. None of this means shit.
Why do we wish to force narrative after every end?
This is only the poet's projection. The severed head
misses nothing, the girl doesn't leave, the boat
continues to sail safely. As for the pig, she remains

dead having met her earthly purposes: to be, to feed, to serve
as female offering. Did you really expect otherwise?
She never enters the ocean in search of herself.
There is no tether, no heroic ghostly hunt.

In death's adjacent room:
let me live inside this girlhood.
He presses his thumbs against
my pulse and I wake beside
the ocean. There is no one
around, except the ladies
pulling oysters from the rock.
They've seen this all before
and will not look, slip
mollusk after mollusk on
their winter-numbed tongues.
Kaleidoscope of faces
and bodies, I know I am lucky
to be living. In another life
I've washed up on shore
halved and picked at by carp.
Above, the sky blots itself antiseptic
pink. I think the worst must be finished.
Whether I am right, don't tell me.
Don't tell me. No ringlet of bruise,
no animal face, the waters salt me
and I leave it barefoot. I leave you, season
of still tongues, of roses on nightstands
beside crushed beer cans. I leave you
white sand and scraped knees. I leave
this myth in which I am pig, whose

death is empty allegory. I leave, I leave—
At the end of this story,
I walk into the sea
and it chooses
not to drown me.

Reversal

Rescind the palm-dash of scallion, the final blessings of ground perilla seeds and sesame leaf. Un-shred the crown daisy. Take the soup off the flame and kill the flame. Un-singe the bottom of the pot until your face reflects in its gunmetal glint. De-Korean the broth: vacate its ginger and onion and garlic. It's rice wine and red swelter. Restore the ground chili flakes to their unshorn forms and hang the bloodless red fruit back up in their perennials. Un-water the perennials, vines retreating to the crease of their seeds. Commit yourself to this un-harvest. To the joy of un-making. Let the soup un-thicken, the starch pull back into the cells of their russets. Fish the russets out from the pork spine cages and lay them to rest back into the earth. Now address the spines. Pick them out from the pot and lay them to grow raw across the cutting board's face. Watch it pull blood back into itself, replenish its own marrow. Love, you'll need your shoes for this. Leave the kitchen. Seek the sow and un-slaughter her. But if you find the pig dismembered and cannot bear it, grant yourself permission to not tend to her re-memberment. Remember: just because you're a daughter doesn't mean you must mend. Instead, let her tend to herself. Her un-thatched belly calling for return of lost things: bone, honeycomb maw, her clumsy animal heart until she speaks; *Dear Reader, I so want to survive this. Please lead me whole into another season so I may dare begin again.*

Grandmother, Praying

Bless this December day, so mild we might finally
undress, drink corn-silk tea cold without shivering.
Bless this home and its four corners, the rice in our bowls
though it is infested. Bless this stone-cut family
so determined not to waste. Bless the weevils,
whole or quartered, peppering the grains,
bori masking the taste, their hard husks
we chew through.

Bless the hen we braised, the rice wine's effervescence.
The milk thistle and stewed burdock, bless them too.
Bless my daughter in her oscillating moods,
her moments of tenderness that set my teeth
aching. Bless my granddaughter,
though she's forsaken you.

Forgive the body, this naked mollusk thing,
I know what it can do. Slit and puncture
wound, I've seen a red sky
escape through. Blue knife of morning, dusk
at comfort stations where girls were halved stone fruit
                    No
        I do not resent you.

Bless the ones still tethered to earth,
who grapple with their own
disappearing. Let them soon reunite
with viscera and bone, forgiven to whole
and rejoice for there are no burning cities
waiting to inherit them.

ACKNOWLEDGMENTS

Warm thanks to the editors of these publications where a number of these poems were first housed, sometimes with different forms or titles:

Adroit: "Savaging"

Blue Mesa Review: "Menstruation Triptych"

BOAAT: "Recipe: 닭도리탕" (Originally published as "Recipe: Chicken Stew") and "Passage, 1951"

Breakwater Review: "Grandmother, Praying" (Originally published as "My Grandmother, Praying")

The Columbia Review: "The Leaving Season"

Fugue: "Blood Type," "Praise," and "Some Are Always Hungry"

Hunger Mountain: "Benediction as Disdained Cuisine"

Narrative Magazine: "All Female" (Originally published as "The Crab")

Prelude: "I Revisit Myself in 1996" (Originally published as "I Revisit Age Four") and "Mother Undresses" (Originally published as "My Mother, Undressing")

Ruminate: "Homonyms"

The Southeast Review: "Diptych of Girl in 1953" (Originally published as "Diptych of My Great Aunt in 1953")

Western Humanities Review: "Saga of the Nymph and the Woodcutter"

New Delta Review: "Diptych of Animal and Womb" (Originally published as "Self Portrait Diptych as Animal and Womb") and "Yellow Fever"

Poetry Northwest: "The Daughter Transmorphic"

Bat City Review: "Field Notes from My Grandparents" (Originally published as "Fragments from My Grandparents")

Winter Tangerine Review: "Fish Head Soup"

Print Oriented Bastards: "Bone Soup, 1951"

Elastic Magazine: "The Tale of Janghwa and Hongryeon"

Tinderbox: "Lilith" and "Thirst"

Muse/ A: "Caught"

Cosmonauts Avenue: "Immigration," and "War Soup"

Timber: "For Now, Nothing Burns" (Originally published as "For Now, Nothing Burning") and "Revisitations"

I am also grateful to the editors of the following anthologies in which some of the poems have been included: *Best New Poets* (University of Virginia Press), *They Rise Like a Wave: An Anthology of Asian-American Women Poets* (Blue Oak Press), and *No Tender Fences: An Anthology of Immigrant and First-Generation American Poetry*.

The poem "All Female" was made into a short film by director Damani Brissett in conjunction with the Visible Poetry Project.

The poem "Thirst" incorporates self-translated lyrics from Sim Soo-Bong's 1984 song *Men Are Ships, Women Are Ports* (남자는 배 여자는 항구).

This collection could not have been possible without the support of so many luminous individuals helping me, in myriad ways, to bring it to fruition. My deepest gratitude to the teams at University of Nebraska Press and *Prairie Schooner*. Particularly to Courtney Ocshner, Ashley Strosnider, Jackson Adams, and my editor Kwame Dawes, thank you for your kind support and for granting me the gift of realizing this dream; I will never be able to thank you enough. Gratitude to the final poetry judges of the 2019 Prairie Schooner Poetry Book Prize, Aimee Nezhukumatathil, Hilda Raz, and Ed Madden for looking kindly upon my work when I often don't grant it the same generosity.

Thanks to the Fulbright Program for sponsoring my research year in South Korea during which a number of the poems from this collection were written. Thanks also to my alma maters, University of California, Davis, and New York University. To my teachers who have seen me through various stages in my writing life: Sharon Olds, Deborah Landau, Matthew Rohrer, Joe Wenderoth, Joshua Clover, and Lynn Freed, thank you for believing in my work. All of you made me a better writer; I am honored to have been your student.

The warmest of thanks to my mentor, Yusef Komunyakaa, whose work was so integral in bringing me to poetry. Thank you for your wisdom, for your generosity of time, your kindness, for the conversations about music and family, for impressing upon me the importance of visiting my family's homeland. Your instruction changed my life, and my poems will forever be indebted to you.

Gratitude to Emily Jungmin Yoon for generously translating into Korean the notes addressed to my grandparents in these acknowledgment pages.

To my friends: Chris Han, Jenny Zhao, Angela Lim, O'Neal Wyche, Tita Janna Macol, Victoria Tomlinson, Jieun Yoo and Young Ji Cha as well as both of their families who at points in my life felt like my own. Thank you to all of you for seeing me through the most vulnerable years of my life, for holding me close and pulling me through with laughter and tenderness. You all help me remain in love with this world.

To my friends and hearts in poetry, which is to say life: Nicole Lachat, Dacota Pratt Pariseau, Ocean Vuong, Gerald Sutton and his family, Shamar Hill, Sophia Holtz, Joe Pan, Carlos Williams, Kenneth May, Heloise Afferez, Ama Codjoe, and Alycia Pirmohamed. Without your support this collection could never have drawn breath. Thank you all for your life-giving friendships, for joyous reunions, unexpected postcards and late-night conversations, for offering your eyes and editorial pens to my work no matter how newly formed and breakable. All of you have helped me to be brave in writing and in living. I am so lucky to walk this path with you.

To you, dear reader. Thank you for being by my side in these pages.

And lastly, I want to thank my family to whom this book is dedicated.

To my grandfather: 할아버지, 가족이란 강인한 것이라는 것을, 그리고 슬픔과 좌절 속에서도 타인을 보듬는 방법을 가르쳐 주셔서 감사합니다. 가족의 안위를 지키기 위해 싸워오신 것에 감사드립니다. 앞으로 할아버지를 가슴 더 깊은 곳에 간직하겠습니다.

To my grandmother: 할머니, 언제나 저를 따스하게 대해주시고 아낌없이 수많은 이야기를 풀어주신 것에 감사드립니다. 저희가 더 행복한 삶을 살 수 있도록 희생하신 모든 것도 감사합니다. 할머니의 목소리가 저의 시 여러 편에 녹아있습니다. 할머니께 영원히 갚을 수 없는 빚을 졌습니다.

And finally, for my mother, the greatest hero of my life. Everything I know of love and of beauty, I learned from you. Mama, your only daughter will be fine, please live in pursuit of your own happiness now.

IN THE PRAIRIE SCHOONER BOOK PRIZE IN POETRY SERIES

Cortney Davis, *Leopold's Maneuvers*
Rynn Williams, *Adonis Garage*
Kathleen Flenniken, *Famous*
Paul Guest, *Notes for My Body Double*
Mari L'Esperance, *The Darkened Temple*
Kara Candito, *Taste of Cherry*
Shane Book, *Ceiling of Sticks*
James Crews, *The Book of What Stays*
Susan Blackwell Ramsey, *A Mind Like This*
Orlando Ricardo Menes, *Fetish: Poems*
R. A. Villanueva, *Reliquaria*
Jennifer Perrine, *No Confession, No Mass*
Safiya Sinclair, *Cannibal*
Susan Gubernat, *The Zoo at Night*
Luisa Muradyan, *American Radiance*
Aria Aber, *Hard Damage*
Jihyun Yun, *Some Are Always Hungry*

To order or obtain more information on these or other University of Nebraska Press titles, visit nebraskapress.unl.edu.

Printed in the USA
CPSIA information can be obtained
at www.ICGtesting.com
LVHW051814061123
763196LV00005B/680